An Agent

A Pocket Guide for Actors

Copyright © 2019 by Natalie Payne

All rights reserved. No part of this book may be reproduced or used in any manner without written permission of the copyright owner.

First Edition: May 2019

The information in this book is based on the personal experiences and viewpoint of the author. All recommendations are made without guarantee and the author disclaims any liability in connection with the use of this information.

CONTENTS

1. FINDING AN AGENT — 1
2. CHOOSING AN AGENT — 20
3. AUDITIONS — 28
4. ACTOR/AGENT RELATIONSHIP — 47
5. THE DREAM CLIENT — 61
6. LEAVING AN AGENT — 68
7. OTHER FAQ'S — 82
ABOUT THE AUTHOR — 96

1. FINDING AN AGENT

Where to start?

Actors need to assess what kind of work they want to be doing, be realistic about their experience, research agencies by whatever means they have available and listen to feedback from others in the industry they respect and have access to. Researching agencies is an important part of the process - getting the fundamentals right early on will increase your options down the line, and the likelihood of you approaching the most suitable agencies and getting positive responses.

> "What works for you, may not work for someone else so your own research is important."

* * *

What should actors be looking out for?

Each actor has to assess their own needs first and foremost, what works for you may not work for someone else. As an agent, it is more beneficial to me if an actor who contacts me for representation already knows a bit about me and the agency, and knows the kind of work my clients are doing. All of these things should be relatively easy to find through websites, social media and word of mouth. They should also know if they have the kind of professional experience that is in tune with the actors I already represent. If not, can they prove that they have the potential to work at that level.

Other things to consider are the size of the agency as it directly affects how you will be represented. There are exceptions in all agencies but typically, larger agencies *could* mean that you will be speaking to multiple people on any given week whereas the smaller the agency, the higher the likelihood you will have a smaller network of team members to call on. The flip side could be that the contacts of the smaller agency "may" be compromised. Things are not always as black and white as they seem in regard to larger/smaller agencies which is why research is so important. I decided to maintain a small list but as my clients become more established, I build a team around them with worldwide agency alliances, for example.

You should look at how many clients the

agent has on their list too, having a larger number of clients will spread an agent's time more thinly and therefore *could* make them less available to you.

I would also avoid the train of thought of looking for actors similar in looks to yourself on an agent's client list. Every actor has context and a unique set of skills and experiences that will be different to yours - if you don't want someone else to pigeon-hole you on looks alone, try not to do it to yourself. It will of course sometimes be relevant and you will of course sometimes be up against "similar looking" actors as the role dictates, but know that what you bring to the table will always be unique and try not to focus on "similar" clients without knowing any back story, because if there isn't a space for you in the agency, then the agent wouldn't be considering you.

> "Know that what you bring to the table will always be unique, so try not to focus on an agency's *similar* clients."

You won't be able to decipher all of this in your research but they are things worth considering at this stage so you can build on your expectations from the beginning. Ultimately, you are assessing an agent as much as the agency and whether you feel you are on the same page and could work together through all of the stages of your career, through good times and bad.

* * *

What do I send to an agent when requesting representation?

All agents/agencies will have different preferences on this, but I like it to be simple. CV, small headshot (under 1mb) and a link to a showreel and/or details of a performance I can watch you in. Ideally, I'd just prefer up to date Spotlight/IMDB links instead of a CV and headshot because I prefer links over attachments. Also, be aware that there may also be restrictions on the agency's incoming email size limits, and therefore your enquiry could be rejected for exceeding that limit if you send an email with multiple attachments. Additional material can always be sent later on by request. As far as a cover letter goes, I like a brief summary of your stand-out skills and jobs and why the agency appeals to you. Hardcopies in the post to the office are not very efficient these days as you can get access to information a lot faster and more efficiently when it's all together electronically, but I know some agents still like postal submissions.

> "Avoid sending multiple attachments with your enquiries. Additional

An Agent's Perspective

==material can always be sent later on if requested."==

This kind of information should, in theory, be made obvious on an agency's website, however a quick call to check preference for submissions is reasonable if nothing is listed. My agency receives a lot of submissions from actors who haven't read the requirements on the website nor have they sent to the correct email address listed. These do not get the same attention as the ones that provide the requested information, the way we like to receive it.

❋ ❋ ❋

Natalie Payne

Things to avoid in cover letters:

- Bad mouthing your current agent (this also applies to conversation in your new agent interviews!) - it reflects badly on your character. By all means say you're unhappy with the amount of quality auditions you've had or that you've found communication difficult (if that's the case), but try not to make blanket negative statements like "my agent is not very good" or "my agent doesn't have the contacts to get me in the room" - it may be your opinion, but it shows a lack of professional integrity and is disrespectful to say to a relative stranger at the offset of communication. It is also a small industry and

An Agent's Perspective

you could be talking about a colleague/friend of the agent you've written to/are meeting with.

- Please don't build up your role in Spielberg's last film, only to not have any evidence of it in the way of footage, IMDB listing, press cuttings, trailers etc. It just makes us not trust your experience and discredits everything else you've done. If you don't have footage or can't get it, it is inadvisable to use that as the main selling point in your cover letter because we would question the size of the role automatically if you were unable to show us some of it. Unless of course you have booked a notable role in an upcoming show that isn't out yet or hasn't opened (theatre). In which case, absolutely mention and send some press release links for context if available.

❊ ❊ ❊

Do you have any practical CV tips?

•   Keep your Spotlight and CV credits up to date. Most recent job at the top.

•   Don't lie about your credits/skills/languages. It's one thing to develop some juggling or horse-riding skills when a role requires it and be "open to learning new skills very quickly" - it's another to sell yourself to an agent on skills you don't

An Agent's Perspective

have. It's not helpful.

- A brief sentence is useful above your credits on a CV/Spotlight if you're mid-job. Be sure to specify when it finishes though so we know when you're fully available from.

- Be realistic with you're playing age. Down and up 5 years is reasonable if you look young/old for your age. If you're claiming more than that, it's wise to seek other opinions _that you can rely on to be honest with you_, so that you can make sure you legitimately look the ages you're stating!

- Recent headshots. If you're using 10-

year-old headshots, it's as unhelpful as an inaccurate playing age because you are being called in under a false pretence. It's in your interest to look like your headshot so no one is surprised when you turn up (this applies to agent meetings and castings alike).

- Professional headshots. These are the first thing agents/casting see most of the time and amateur shots stand out for all of the wrong reasons. This is a necessary investment.

❋ ❋ ❋

How do I stand out?

An Agent's Perspective

If I see talent alongside good credits then I will always be intrigued. I could compromise on most things for exceptional talent so *proving* your talent will make you stand out. There will be plenty of time to chat later on about why you got into acting and your dream roles for the future, I don't look for this in an initial email. It certainly doesn't need to be all factual with no heart, but just not so wordy that the key information is lost. If you are sending a CV and headshot blindly with no upcoming shows/showreel/recent self-tapes, and you know the agent hasn't seen you perform recently, then I'd recommend waiting until you do have those things before writing in, because realistically the chances of being considered for representation by a reputable agent are slim on CV and email alone.

> "Cover letters should not be so wordy that the key information is lost."

* * *

Is it realistic to expect an agent to come and watch me if I invite them to a production?

Yes, it's realistic, but it's also completely dependent on the agent's needs at the time and whether they think you are a good fit for the agency. I couldn't possibly

An Agent's Perspective

go to everything I was invited to, for example, and if I'm not looking to add clients to my list then I don't put much time aside for watching potential new clients as I am busy managing and supporting my client list, but there are occasionally exceptions to the rule if I get excited by someone and want to see more. I will however always try and watch the emerging talent at the drama schools because I want to see who is about for the future. Because industry demands change all the time, so do the needs of the agency.

Should I follow up after I have sent my submission?

If I am interested and have an opening we will usually reach out to an actor within a month of receiving a CV – there are occasions where it has taken longer but that is not the norm. It would be nice to reply to everyone personally, but we wouldn't have time for anything else and would risk compromising time spent on existing clients. I'd rather actors didn't follow up on submissions (exceptions *could* be if I know the actor personally or they have been recommended by someone I know very well) because we just don't have time to respond to follow-ups all day, and the chances of having a fruitful conversation/remembering your submission/seeking out your CV after a phone call, when we are juggling multiple other things for the existing clients is unlikely. Just send a well-thought-out submission through and if an agent is interested, they will get in touch with you relatively quickly regardless of whether you follow up or not.

It's worth noting that an agent may think you are a brilliant actor but sometimes the timing just isn't right to consider you for representation. Don't let that deter you from approaching other agencies who may have a space or even trying again down the line.

2. CHOOSING AN AGENT

What can I expect of an actor/agent interview?

I want to find out about your career to date, who you have existing working relationships with (in the way of casting directors, producers, directors etc) and what you are like as a person, because I'm trying to assess whether we can work together and get along in the process. If I've invited you for interview then chances are I've already seen you perform or seen a strong showreel, usually both, so there will rarely be the need to perform at the meeting. It doesn't hurt to have a couple of key questions written down and if they haven't been answered through the conversation then it's usual that an actor would want to ask them. I have had many actors bring in questions which I don't mind at all, I think it shows that they have really thought about the meeting and want to get the most out of it. Just bear in mind it's a conversation and more than likely your main queries will be answered during it, so let it happen organically knowing you have the safety net of some questions that are important to you in the back of your mind, or written down just in case.

It's always helpful to take a print out of your CV and headshot/Spotlight CV with you as well. I sometimes like to go through these (literally or just by way of conversation) in a meeting in case there are any points to discuss, such as interesting skills and roles, and also to check the headshots are recent and a true likeness. It also makes you look well-prepared and professional to have these with you even if it doesn't come up.

An Agent's Perspective

✻ ✻ ✻

Should an actor feel they have to accept an offer there and then, or is it okay to go away and have a think, or perhaps see other agents before making a decision on representation?

I think it makes sense to see all of the agents that are interested that you like and to take your time in making a decision. But saying that, if you wait too long, the agent may think you are not interested or taking the offer seriously so will move on. I would just be open and ask about a timescale – say you have other agents to meet with and will decide when you have met them all. If the agent likes you they will wait, but if an agent senses you are just biding your time until you find a "better" agent, then it's a bad start and it's probably not going to work out.

> "Be open and honest about your expectations and you will (hopefully) be met with the same."

Bear in mind not every actor that an agent meets with will be offered representation either, so just be open and honest about your expectations and you will (hopefully) be met with the same.

✽ ✽ ✽

What happens next?

If you are both happy with moving forward there is usually an agreement for both parties to sign outlining the contractual obligations on either side. This will be case by case depending on the agency, but if you are worried about the contract aspect of signing with an agent then seek independent advice as with any other contract. The key things to look out for are commission rates, length of contract and what happens if it's not working out down the line and you part ways.

✼ ✼ ✼

What happens in the initial period after signing?

This is completely dependent on the actor, their level of experience and the individual methods of the agent/s you've started working with. However, in an ideal world, current projects and roles will be discussed and you will both be in a situation of wanting to get auditioning straight away. The initial few months are a great time to really build the foundations of a strong working relationship and get to know each other and the types of roles the actor is aiming for, so don't be afraid to let us know if a role is not for you. An agent will advise you if they think a role is worth your time but at the same time, you will always have a choice about whether this is a role you want to play. Remember that communication is key so that you can build a successful working partnership from the beginning, and if there's a role you don't want to play or an aspect of a role that makes you uncomfortable, an agent will respect that. If they don't, this is a red flag for future relations and mutual respect and not something to be taken lightly.

❋ ❋ ❋

3. AUDITIONS

How difficult is it to get an audition?

A casting director receives thousands of suggestions (literally) for each role you have been suggested for by your agent (or by you, if you are self-represented). There are usually a handful of auditions available. Add to that the fact you are competing with actors that the producers/director/creative team may know and have

An Agent's Perspective

relationships with, and actors the casting directors know and have cast before. If you are not in that first batch of favourites, sometimes you have to work twice as hard to make an impression should you make it to that handful they see at the audition, until you too have forged your own access on to their radars!

This is not to deter you, this is simply to give some perspective and offer a reality check on opportunities that are available. Auditions should be respected. A busy period does not guarantee a lifelong supply of auditions and a quiet period should not mean that you are not staying focussed and ready.

Natalie Payne

"Auditions should be respected."

✻ ✻ ✻

Do agents/casting directors mind changing days/times of auditions?

They certainly prefer it when you don't! There is a lot of work going on behind the scenes in the lead up to a casting across the board, it doesn't make sense to add more problems to the mix if you can help it. It's one thing for us to move things around commitments we know about and are aware of at the point of fighting for an

An Agent's Perspective

audition (much easier and less disruptive to the process), it's another to drop bombshells we're unaware of when we book in a meeting. It's exhausting and makes us think you're not as committed as other clients/actors that would relish the opportunity.

In short, it implies:

- You've not told us you were unavailable.
- You're prioritising other commitments over your acting.
- You're not as committed as other actors.
- You don't recognise or appreciate the opportunity.

If you are not recognising the opportunity and supporting the process, then there's only so much anyone can do. Not liking/wanting the role is a different discussion of course as is flexibility for off-peak travel to lessen the cost of a meeting. These are absolutely a few circumstances that agents/casting will understand and work to (if able). Although ideally, these will have been communicated previously so everyone knows any restrictions in advance.

Ultimately, auditions are for the actor to have a chance at an acting role – they are a good thing (it feels crazy emphasising this but sometimes when agents get so many initial reactions about how inconveniently timed a meeting may be, it starts to make us question if clients actually want it, and we are wasting our time fighting their corner).

Time and day often become the focus but I think that should be secondary to the audition itself; the project, the role, the potential of the role, who you'll be meeting etc.

> "Be the solution to the problem, not another problem in the matrix of the casting process."

Natalie Payne

❋ ❋ ❋

What kinds of auditions can I expect?

"In the room" auditions – for screen roles, this *typically* means you will be auditioning with casting in person with some pre-prepared material in the way of script/sides as needed. The casting director (or their associate/assistant) will typically read opposite you and the audition will likely be taped for future reference/other members of the team. Theatre auditions are not usually filmed. These are usually held in a casting studio/rehearsal room.

"Self-tape" auditions – usually for screen roles (occasionally stage roles allow for tapes but this is less common). This *typically* involves filming the audition yourself at home with a smart phone/camera and using a friend/family member/colleague to read the other lines for you off-camera. You would then send the finished tape to your agent in a downloadable format via WeTransfer/Hightail and the like, or a downloadable (private) link to a streaming site such as Vimeo/Dropbox (preferences will vary). If everyone is happy with the quality of the tape, your agent would then send it on to casting by their preferred method.

"Recalls" (sometimes called "call-backs") – for stage/screen roles. Any time you are called in after the initial audition will be a recall (could follow either of the above), usually "in the room" and with typically more members of the creative team in addition to casting. There will sometimes be additional scenes to prepare and sometimes some notes to take on from any previous meetings. There can sometimes be a number of recalls for a given job. Usually with existing and/or new material and in front of additional creative team members as the process goes on. There are various types of recalls at later stage auditions to include work sessions, director sessions, producer sessions, screen tests, studio tests, network tests. *Typically,* the

An Agent's Perspective

further you get into a process, the more in contention you are and the more people you have to perform for.

"Chemistry read" – Mainly for screen roles but sometimes stage roles. This is typically a later stage audition whereby they want to see if there is any chemistry between other actors that have already been cast, or with actors that are being considered to look at how different pairings/groups work together. Usually with 1 or more other actors working more closely on existing and/or new material. This is usually filmed and many members of the creative team will be present.

There could be various other potential

interactions through a casting process depending on logistics/various other practicalities. These could include **phone calls, video calls, informal face to face meetings** etc.

The increased use of technology has opened up so many extra ways for actors to be considered for a role, so be prepared to use all options you have available to you should the situation call for it!

❋ ❋ ❋

Pre-audition nerves?

Sometimes, productions have been in de-

An Agent's Perspective

velopment for years before the point of audition. From the companies putting their money on the line through to the writers, production teams and casting directors – everyone has their own job to do to ensure the success of a production and everyone wants to do it well. I think it's important, and perhaps helpful, for actors to recognise that everyone else in the audition room will have their own pressures relating to their involvement in the production, whether it be the writer who is worried about their script being in question; the casting director hoping that the actors they've called in will impress the creative team etc. So, they will absolutely be rooting for you to solve their problem and make the production a success as much as you would want to solve it and be cast, because that reflects well on them too! It may help to focus on this when the nerves set in.

> "Think of yourself as the missing piece to the casting puzzle and know that you both need each other for success."

❋ ❋ ❋

When will I hear back after an audition?

Casting a role can take days or months

An Agent's Perspective

and in some (albeit less common) cases, years! Hopefully you'll get a rough idea of time scale by the production dates and any pre-given recall dates but sometimes, you won't have a clear timescale to work to. If they like you, they usually give an incline relatively quickly but then I've also known casting to go completely silent for months and then re-appear (this could be down to any number of things such as loss of funding, they cast the role but need to re-look at actors they liked previously for a re-cast, dates were put back etc). Very often, we don't hear anything at all if it's not going any further, especially early on in the casting process in the "first rounds".

❋ ❋ ❋

My agent rarely gets me proper feedback from my audition, why not?

This is something I hear a lot from actors and I understand the frustration on lack of audition feedback. I think it's important to remember that agents are sometimes just the messenger and if there is no message given, they have nothing to relay. Please know that we all want feedback for you – agents also want to know why it's not going any further and whether there is anything we can do differently from our side to help you book next time. Likewise, it's just helpful to know whether it's a reason that is out of all of our control.

There has been a great campaign recently that demands a #YesorNo from casting after a meeting. I fully support this campaign and getting a "no" allows an actor (and agents) to park an audition and move on. Casting directors however, are under a lot of pressure to complete on casting for a project and they won't always have time to let every actor they have seen know they are not taking things any further. It's not ideal and of course we would all love in depth feedback after each session to be able to learn from it (if able) ahead of the next one, but I think the most we can hope for after a first audition or a tape is a no (where there is no recall/role offered). Feedback is hard to get without obstructing a casting director's day (if every agent called for feedback the day after a thirty actor audition day for example, no one would have time for anything else), and realistically you'd probably rather an agent only called casting to push you for a role than keep pressing them on roles you didn't get, for feedback that will likely be quite generic at that point because of the sheer volume of actors being considered.

I typically don't expect feedback after one audition or tape but the further into a process an actor gets, the more specific feedback can be and the more willing casting directors are to give it to agents/actors. I do hope that a "no" is given as standard more often than it is now going forward though – it would make all of our lives a little easier and show respect for the work done by actors/agents in the lead up to the meeting. But if I had to choose between more auditions and opportunities for actors or a reluctantly given piece of feedback, I think the auditions are more valuable to us so I try to focus on the silver lining where possible.

> "Self-belief is so important in times where feedback is sparse."

One way that could help retain sanity (after an audition) is to focus on the elements that you can control up until that point, know that you prepped and did the best you can with what you had available, and then it will be easier (in theory) to draw a line under a meeting after you leave the room. Feedback is a bonus. And if a recall or offer doesn't come through, you will at least know you gave a good audition based on your own instincts. Some things will always be outside of our control and outside of what happens in the audition room and sometimes, as difficult as it is, we just have to accept that there may be no tangible reason why it didn't go your way and trust in our respective abilities - self-belief is so important in times where feedback is sparse.

❋ ❋ ❋

4 ACTOR/ AGENT RELATIONSHIP

How often should you call your agent to 'touch base'?

My clients know if I need to talk to them

about a part or send them a script to look over I will. If you "touch base" every few weeks it's fine but bear in mind that if they've not called it is likely that there is nothing significant to discuss…

❀ ❀ ❀

Out of sight, out of mind?

No. Agents work every day on their client's behalf. It's not in anyone's interest to not do that job given that they are not paid for their time until an actor secures a role. Instead of asking what your agent is doing every day, it is more helpful to look at what you can be doing to be ready. Honing your craft, exercising your skills and researching roles for example. That is your job. Let agents do theirs. Actors/agents should be a team, I don't think it should feel like a hierarchy from either perspective – both are important and both should be respected in their roles.

❋ ❋ ❋

What do agents do every day?

Read scripts, discuss scripts, discuss roles, suggest for roles, negotiate deals, read contracts, amend contracts, re-amend contracts, make dates work, fight to make dates work, schedule auditions, fight to make clashing auditions work, quality check your self-tapes, edit and upload your self-tapes for casting, talk to or take meetings with casting directors/writers/producers/directors about their projects, talk to affiliate representatives across different time zones, talk to/meet with clients, advise clients, give good news, give bad news, attend press events, attend plays/screenings, discuss said plays and screenings, organise your publicity interviews/premieres/charity events/PA's in the event of no publicist, update websites/IMDB/Spotlight as needed, monitor socials…….

❋ ❋ ❋

What agents don't do?

Sit at the desk leisurely submitting clients on breakdowns all day and not much else!

I think it's important to acknowledge the amount of work being done behind the scenes for clients and how much pressure agents are under, as much as I think it's important for agents to appreciate the extreme pressure actors are under each day staying motivated and sharing control over something so important to them. Not to mention the obvious pressures of auditioning, the uncertainty between jobs, and the pressure to be on top form during jobs.

As long as you are making the most of the time you do have between acting jobs, including putting in extra hours around any second jobs or other acting roles then you know that you are doing everything that you can be doing to be ready. And rest assured, your agents will be doing that also. If you are not auditioning at all (despite having provided your agent with all available ammunition for them to fight for you e.g. great headshots, showreel etc.) and if you don't have faith in your agent's work ethic or contacts, then seek a new agent.

An Agent's Perspective

> "Control the things you can control so you can be ready for the things you can't."

✷ ✷ ✷

Should you rely on your agent for all of your work, or do agents encourage clients to get out there looking for their own work?

It's important to stay proactive generally speaking. Fringe plays/festivals even though the money is lower are a great thing to do to keep skills sharp and stay creative, but they shouldn't be the sole focus nor conflict with auditions and paid work. Equally, if not more so, is maintaining skillset and staying creative whether that be writing, producing own work, working on accents, attending workshops, practicing self-taping. Your skills, and what you work on outside of the audition rooms and in between jobs is part of the job in my opinion; controlling the things you can control so you can be ready for the things you can't.

❋ ❋ ❋

If you do find your own work, do you still have to pay your agent for that

job?

Remember that your agent is on your team. All team members want you to be working and are actively trying to make this happen on a daily basis. This is as much about principle as it is about the agent's commission.

If a client were to accept a job without discussing it with me or my team at all, I would argue that there is a huge communication breakdown in the relationship and a lack of respect for the work being done by the agent (even when an actor isn't working). Accepting a job without discussion (regardless of commission) affects availability, auditions that are pending, active projects that your agent is working on for you etc.

Secondly, finding and creating opportunities is one part of what an agent is doing on a daily basis; the professional advice, guidance and support through the stages of securing a job, negotiating the best possible deal, through the rehearsal stages, performances, previews, press nights, screenings, premieres (and beyond!) are a few others. Not wanting to pay commission or even divulge a direct enquiry, aside from the fact that it would hugely affect the integrity of the relationship, would certainly compromise willingness of the agent to have professional involvement through the job.

An Agent's Perspective

Thirdly, most agency contracts usually specify that all acting work be put through the agency while under representation – even where an actor is contacted directly. You could be in breach of contract if you keep a job secret or decide not to pay commission due. But this would depend on the agreement you have made with your agent.

And finally, and importantly, it's in the actor's interest to forward direct enquiries, not only because it keeps things professional with the person who contacted you, but the agent can negotiate the best possible deal and keep the actor's interests and other commitments at the forefront of conversations. If your natural instinct is to deal with something yourself and not put it through the agent and communicate with them about it, then that's the start of a slippery slope to an ineffective working relationship. It also implies that you don't value their involvement in your career, in which case, it may be time to leave your agent and manage your acting jobs independently.

> "It's in the actor's interest to forward direct enquiries."

* * *

What is the most important part of

the actor/agent relationship and how can you ensure that it has the best chance of success?

Just be honest, professional and keep the lines of communication open but also trust that your agent is working even when it feels quiet to you. If you lose that trust or don't feel you can communicate openly (and have tried) then it's time to look for alternative representation because it's probably not the right fit for you.

The mutual goal is to create a rock-solid foundation underneath your acting career and a strong level of understanding that allows you to focus on your acting, knowing that you have a trusted professional ally through the mayhem.

✻ ✻ ✻

5. THE DREAM CLIENT

The actor-agent relationship is a partnership. From the beginning when the actor is new and developing, through to the point an actor has some success, through to international recognition! If the balance of the scales remains on a level throughout then I believe it benefits everyone.

There should be no hierarchy regardless of where someone is at in their career, just a mutual respect, honesty and trust (which all will benefit from).

On a more practical level, here is my "dream client" wish list:

- Prioritising acting roles above second jobs

Second jobs are important (and sometimes crucial) to fund the acting where the roles are too infrequent to live off, but should not be so restrictive that they stop you auditioning for roles entirely, or cause too much inflexibility on times/days. It will annoy casting directors and agents alike and could restrict future opportunities.

- Always arriving in good time to auditions
- Always well prepared
- Respectful
- Professional
- Good communication
- Doesn't text/call an agent's mobile out of hours for anything that isn't urgent

You will get a more fruitful response when an agent is engaged in the conversation and this will happen in reasonable hours during the working week. Save it up, put it on an email and leave their mobile for emergencies or reasonable hours only.

- Mutual trust and respect for job roles

"Checking in" constantly and asking for a list of suggestions on a regular basis plants the seed of distrust – it's like asking your agent if they're doing their job properly. In the same way I wouldn't keep calling my clients to check they're working on their accents/skillset/staying sharp every day, I expect the same by return. Granted, if something needs discussing e.g. you've been sent another role you hate and therefore want to discuss other roles you're up for with that in mind, it's relevant and important for both parties. Likewise, if your accent slipped on a recent tape, and the agent flags it up, communication on

An Agent's Perspective

the issue will need to happen until it's resolved and suggestions/roles you're up for will likely be adjusted until it's up to standard. These are normal lines of communication.

- Good quality recent headshots (that look like you).
- Good quality showreel footage

Some actors still do not have showreels despite years of professional experience, there is no excuse if you are serious about your career. Why wouldn't you want to put yourself in the best possible position and arm your agent/yourself with as many tools as possible to help you stand out. Words on a page can only do so much with the best will and contacts in the world.

> "A showreel doesn't need an elaborate montage to be effective."

If you do not have the experience for a showreel then I would suggest doing what it takes to get it and taking it seriously. Short films, self-taping scenes etc. are also helpful. There are always options available if you look for them and you shouldn't need to spend a fortune. A basic iMovie edit can be done for free if you have some professional footage – it may require a bit of time and effort to learn but it's a good skill to hone and worth your time. Also, some agencies will also be happy to cut scenes together for you. A showreel doesn't need an elaborate montage to be effective.

I think it's important that actors take control where they are able to in this industry even if it means learning some basic skills outside of the acting remit, especially in the early days when there are minimal credits and roles to speak of. An increased level of understanding will always be useful.

❋ ❋ ❋

6. LEAVING AN AGENT

What is the best way to go about leaving your agent?

I think if we behave in a way that is honest, open and respectful then we deserve that back – leaving your agent is no exception.

And this also rings true when it comes to releasing a client.

※ ※ ※

Should I let an agent know I'm leaving before I've found another agent?

There are a few trains of thoughts on this ranging from being honest with your agent before you approach new agents to finding a new agent before you tell your current one to cover yourself. If you respect your agent but don't feel the professional relationship is working then a discussion with them should have happened at some point to address the issues. If nothing changes after this discussion then another one should happen to end the working relationship. It is likely if you are feeling it's not working, they are on the same page and you can mutually see out any notice period or agree to call it a day without any dis-respect or bad feeling.

If you're ending the relationship because it's not working then will it matter if they're not representing you while you search elsewhere? If you are not open about things, then all it does it fuel bad blood. But alas, I'd say most actors that approach me for representation are with other agents and only a very small percentage say that their agent is aware they are looking elsewhere so it is your prerogative.

It is possible to end an actor-agent relationship with relations in tact but it more than likely won't come after testing the water with their colleagues over the road or slating them in a meeting or to industry colleagues – it's a smaller industry than you think and people talk. Amicable, professional and respectful endings are the best kind. This goes both ways of course. Integrity counts for a lot and it is something we can choose to maintain on both sides.

❋ ❋ ❋

Do I need to change agents when I start landing bigger roles?

It is one thing to leave an agent because the relationship/communication has broken down and you're not being seen for quality roles – it is another altogether to leave when things are going well. A lot of this depends on a person's character and a recognition of the team effort involved booking roles and, in the agent/client relationship.

If you have had a great year/s with your current agent and are pleased with the roles you are working on and reading for, it seems bizarre to me that an actor would look for alternative representation – yes, even if the agent to a Hollywood star tracks you down. It shows a lack of recognition for work done and a lack of faith in your agent (which is unfounded if you are already working and happy). Everyone will have their own views on what an agent can and can't do for you and people will exert their opinions onto you throughout you career on who the "best" agents are. There are good and bad agents in big and small agencies so you can only really fully trust your own personal experiences and judgement to know what is right for you.

❋ ❋ ❋

Some reasons to leave your current agent:

- You are not able to communicate effectively with each other.
- They are consistently sending you for roles that you have expressed a desire not to be seen for.
- You are not getting the level of audition that your experience should warrant.
- You are not auditioning at all for an extended period of time without explanation or reason.
- They behave in a way that makes you feel uncomfortable or dis-respected.

Some reasons <u>not</u> to leave your agent:

- You are auditioning for roles you would like to play.
- They understand you, your range of acting, your skillset, roles you like/dislike.
- You have history and therefore a level of understanding that will take time to develop with a new agent.
- You have had a run of success booking roles.
- You have had a run of near misses on roles.

To flip the perspective, here are some reasons an agent may not wish to work with you anymore:

- You go off-radar and we cannot reach you.
- You are consistently late for auditions.
- You are not fully prepared for an audition.
- You miss deadlines on self-tape auditions consistently.
- You are consistently passing auditions/changing your mind/cancelling last minute.
- You are not able to attend auditions because of your second job i.e. the second job ends up being prioritised over the

acting as opposed to a source of funding to support it.

- Consistently bad availability.
- Disrespectful behaviour.
- Consistently negative attitude.
- Frequent "out of hours" calls/texts.
- You still don't have that showreel we've been promised for years.
- You still haven't invested in new headshots despite multiple requests and looking nothing like your current ones.

Context is crucial here. If the reason you haven't booked is for any of the reasons directly above then there is only so much an agent can do and it's necessary for the actor to take responsibility. On the flip side if you have just been unlucky/are getting close to roles but are otherwise professional and committed then not many agents would release a client at this point. This is where loyalty and respect come in and a level of understanding. Saying that, if years go by and an actor doesn't book a role or even come close, there is only so long anyone can keep working unpaid, with the best will in the world, everyone has bills to pay. And ultimately, some agent's thresholds of time are longer than others.

❖ ❖ ❖

Practically speaking, what happens when I leave an agency/or I am re-

leased as a client?

You will need to check your contracts/agreements (formal or otherwise) for what was agreed in the event of the working relationship ending first and foremost as this will be different in each case. Some agencies have a notice period applied both sides – whether you are giving it or them.

As an example, let's say you have a period of a month where you are still under contract with your existing agent, this will *typically* mean that all auditions, jobs and contracts started over this period (and naturally anything before it) would warrant commission to your existing agent.

Furthermore, if you secure a role in this time and it has options attached to it e.g. for future series/films in the same role, those options/contracts would *typically* go through your existing agent even if those options are not exercised until sometime later (unless the option is not obligatory and you turn it down or there is some other exception to the rule). Either way, it is wise to let any new agent know about existing options you have on a contract (for example) as this will directly affect your availability to the new agent and means that they may not be entitled to any commission on that job. This can be a deterrent to some agents. It could also be an incentive if the role is high profile enough to justify the period of no commission. Trying to withhold this kind of information entirely however will certainly set your new partnership off to a shaky start!

So, in short, just be frank about anything that you think could be an issue. They may not be issues at all, but they may also be contractual obligations.

> "Communicate what you know, question what you don't and remain open with any new agents that you are meeting with/joining."

❋ ❋ ❋

7. OTHER FREQUENTLY ASKED QUESTIONS

Do agents have time to mentor their new actors?

If you are green on industry standards and auditions, it's in an agent's interest to make sure you are equipped with some knowledge and to impart any useful pearls of wisdom to help steer you in the right direction over those initial few months (and beyond) until you feel more sure of various scenarios. It's important that you build a strong foundation for the working relationship so actors should not be afraid to ask questions on anything they're unsure about – it's crucial actually. An agent is on your team and wants you to succeed as much as you do.

❋ ❋ ❋

Natalie Payne

How difficult is it to get new actors out there and working right now? Do you find that a lot of casting directors/producers/directors have their own wish lists of established artists or are people open to taking risks on new talent?

There will always be the demand for well-known faces in a show, on stage and screen, because audiences like to watch people they recognise and have enjoyed before. It will generally be "easier" in that there will be a greater choice of roles if you are well-known or established because that's how the industry is and the more experience you build, the more chance you have of getting into that bracket yourself. And of course, every now and then there are roles that are easier for casting and production to look further afield and give emerging actors a chance on – in fact there are roles where emerging actors are the focus of a casting. But, to clarify, you don't need to be well-known to the world to be respected within the industry. There will (hopefully) always be roles for talented, hard-working actors both known and unknown, so there's no point focussing too much on the elements of the industry that are out of your control and just be ready for the things you can be ready for.

"You don't need to be well-known to the world to be respected within the industry"

After all, every well-known actor was an unknown one at one point, and every established actor had a point when they had one credit on their CV, so you have to be prepared to start at the bottom and work for what you want. There will be an element of luck that propels some actors faster than others into their dream roles but that shouldn't deter you or act as a reason to be resentful or cynical. That's their journey (and it also has its pitfalls) and you will have your own.

An Agent's Perspective

> "Work hard, and stay ready for the next opportunity because it will probably come when you least expect."

✱ ✱ ✱

Actors are very aware of their 'Hit Rate', or ratio of auditions to being booked for the job. What is acceptable and when does an agent become concerned that something might be wrong?

This will always be a case by case scenario. I wouldn't be concerned if my client had had ten auditions and not booked one of them if the feedback was typically positive and/or they're getting some recalls and good momentum – there are a lot of factors at play that none of us can control and sometimes it's just not quantifiable with a number or a "hit rate". All that serves to do is add more pressure to an already pressurised situation.

But, I would be concerned if an actor had more than one audition with negative feedback i.e. they were late, hadn't learned their lines, had a bad attitude - because this reflects on me and my agency and the confidence a casting director has in my other clients and suggestions which

I would not accept.

Ultimately, if I have an actor on my books, I believe in their ability and trust they will do their best in the auditions so the main things that will concern me will be how an actor and agent work together, and naturally some pairings work better than others and sometimes it's in both of our interests to end the working relationship.

> "A lot of opportunities are not taken advantage of because an actor wasn't ready – use your time between

jobs/auditions wisely, it's extra rehearsal time."

* * *

When should an actor be concerned with an agent's performance? How many auditions should an actor expect his/her agent to be securing them?

I think there is too much focus around number of auditions. One carefully thought out quality meeting is worth a lot more than five meetings for roles that don't excite you or you're not right for.

Ultimately, there should be a mutual trust – I know I have said this a lot but it is so key. The actor trusts that the agent is putting them through for suitable parts (which is based on communication that has evolved through representation), and the agent trusts that the actor will be prepared and do a good job when it comes to the audition. It's easy to forget that an agent is effectively investing their own time and money day in, day out until an actor secures a job. It's not in an agent's interest to have a non-working actor on the books. If the relationship is not working for whatever reason that is a separate issue that needs to be addressed but, on this question, my focus would be more on the quality of the auditions than the number, and this is gained through an agent's knowledge of their client's abilities, a strong working relationship and a high level of trust on both sides.

> "A team-effort is more beneficial than a dictatorship."

✳ ✳ ✳

Some agents show their clients what they have been put forward for on a monthly basis. If your agent doesn't have time to do this, how do you know your agent is working for you?

An Agent's Perspective

I have covered this briefly already but ultimately, if you don't trust that your agent is working then you are with the wrong agent!

Asking for a "submissions list" all the time is not helpful and quite obstructive – it also shows a lack of trust in your agent which does not bode well for the working relationship. Just as they trust that you are doing the best you can in the audition room and leading up to it (and likewise on jobs), you must trust that they are doing their best in their domain. Although, if there's bad communication and you feel anxious and "in the dark" on a frequent basis, you need to address that with them.

You will ideally have enough communication to know what is going on but not so much that you are taking time away from the agent doing their job. You should also trust that they are suggesting you for appropriate roles based on the relationship and understanding that has been built over time.

> "You will ideally have enough communication to know what is going on but not so much that you are taking time away from the agent doing their job."

An Agent's Perspective

❊ ❊ ❊

ABOUT THE AUTHOR

Natalie Payne has more than 15 years' experience in the Entertainment and Broadcast industry. Having originally trained as a Broadcast Journalist (BJTC accredited), she worked across broadcast journalism, production and post-produc-

An Agent's Perspective

tion at Channel 4, BBC and ITV in her early years before transitioning to working as a talent agent to actors in film, television and theatre in 2007, forming her own agency, Payne Management in 2010.

Natalie built her agency with the focus on investing into discovering newcomers and unknowns in mostly untapped regions of the UK, leading to multiple "Stars of Tomorrow" (Screen International) – the coveted recognition of emerging talent and BAFTA Scholarship winners among her client list.

With worldwide agency alliances, Natalie regularly deals with major UK and US television, film and theatre companies and maintains an eclectic and original list of emerging and established talent.

Find online:

Instagram: @anagentsperspective

www.paynemanagement.co.uk
Twitter: @PayneMgmt
Facebook: /PayneManagement

Natalie Payne Twitter: @Just_Nat

❋ ❋ ❋

Printed in Great Britain
by Amazon